Incredible Stackables:
Ornamental Scroll Saw Projects

Schiffer Publishing Ltd

4880 Lower Valley Road, Atglen, PA 19310 USA

Frank Pozsgai

Dedication

In loving memory of my father-in-law, Paul L. Currin, nicknamed "Beno," for his continuous support of my family.

Copyright © 2001 by Frank Pozsgai
Library of Congress Card Number: 00-111261

Designed by Bonnie M. Hensley
Cover design by Bruce M. Waters
Type set in Dutch801 Rm BT

ISBN: 0-7643-1304-5
Printed in China

Published by Schiffer Publishing Ltd.
4880 Lower Valley Road
Atglen, PA 19310
Phone: (610) 593-1777; Fax: (610) 593-2002
E-mail: Schifferbk@aol.com
Please visit our web site catalog at **www.schifferbooks.com**

In Europe, Schiffer books are distributed by Bushwood Books
6 Marksbury Avenue Kew Gardens
Surrey TW9 4JF England
Phone: 44 (0) 20-8392-8585; Fax: 44 (0) 20-8392-9876
E-mail: Bushwd@aol.com
Free postage in the UK. Europe: air mail at cost.

This book may be purchased from the publisher.
Include $3.95 for shipping. Please try your bookstore first.
We are always looking for people to write books on new and related subjects.
If you have an idea for a book please contact us at the Atglen, PA. address.
You may write for a free catalog.

Contents

Acknowledgments

Many outstanding companies combined efforts to assist Pozsgai's Designs in making this book possible. Questions about equipment and accessories may be directed to: •Woodcrafters, Portland, Oregon; •Penn State Industries, Philadelphia, Pennsylvania; •The Olson Saw Co., Bethel, Connecticut; •The Woodworking Store, Hickey, North Carolina; •Porter Cable Delta Machinery, Jackson, Tennessee; •Wildwood Designs, Inc., Richland Center, Wisconsin; •Meisel Hardware Specialties, Mound, Minnesota; •Amana Tool Corp, Farmingdale, New York.

My thanks goes out to all these fine companies and their helpful people.

Introduction

Incredible Stackables was designed for the both the beginning and the advanced sawyer. The ornamental patterns are at the same time simple enough for everyone and filled with enough potential to challenge the most skilled scroll sawyer. All the patterns are original size and are drawn in outline. However your craft is only limited by your imagination—in how you choose to display them. One can see the numerous ways items can be given used creatively by turning to the Gallery section in this book. Even more, the patterns can also be used to create puzzles for the kids or grandkids...a great learning tool about various animals.

For the sake of all sawyer's we will be adding to any of our future books a complete scroll saw blades selection chart, as well as a general (SPM) blade guide. This information will be very beneficial in improving your knowledge with respect to proper blade selection.

Once again I would appreciate hearing from you about your success with these projects. And please send me any suggestions or requests for future pattern designs. "Happy cuttin' to ya!"

Instructions & Tips

Special Blade and Cutting Hints

- The blade you use should have a minimum of three teeth per material thickness.
- Cutting speeds may be increased using blades with larger teeth, but this will result in a finished edge that will be rougher.
- Finer (smoother) cuts may be achieved with blades with more teeth per inch and slower cutting speeds.
- When cutting soft materials, use a blade with large teeth. Hard materials are cut best with a blade with fine teeth.
- If saw burns or melts material when cutting, either slow the cutting speed or increase the blade size (blades with more teeth).
- One additional tip to reduce or eliminate burning. Using 2" clear 3M packing tape I envelope the wood or simply place the tape over or under the pattern I'm about to cut. The tape lubricates the blade preventing burning. You won't believe your eyes at the results! Use this method with all hard & exotic woods.

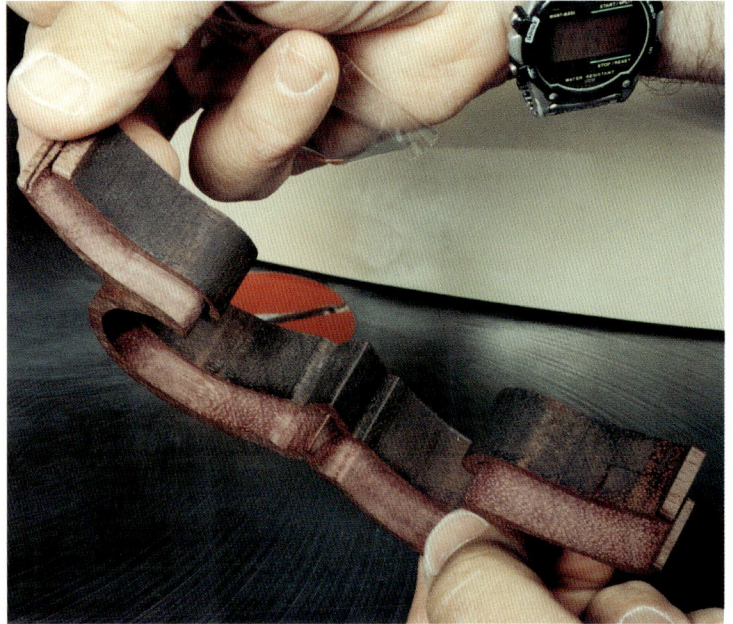

You can see the result of two cuts with the same blade and speed in this piece of purple heart wood. The top one was done without the tape and shows much burning. The bottom one was done with the tape in place.

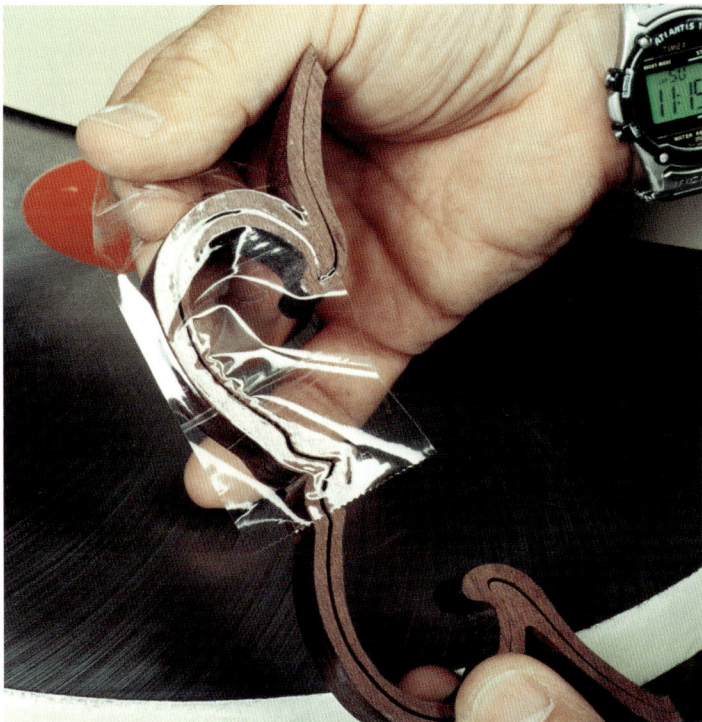

This purple heart wood burns very easily, particularly with the tight scroll work you see on this piece. By apply clear packing tape before cutting, it is possible to reduce or eliminate the burning.

The Right Blade For The Right Job

Contrary to numerous opinions, just like mine, it's the end result of what one achieves with the scroll saw that counts. I am repeatedly asked "what blade should I use?" There are too many variables to consider to give a pat answer to that question! The saw itself whether it's an Excalibur, a Hegner, Delta, RBI Hawk, or an import, is not the most important factor. Most saws can be made to do a good job. More important factors are the blade tension, the feed rate, your sensitivity, the speed (SPM), and the type of material you are cutting.

That being said, the blade is the single most important component of a scroll saw! If the right blade is not used for the job, the results won't be worth anything. And there are so many variables that you need to have a variety of blades available for your saw. Remember that one or two common blades will not be enough for a novice, much less the accomplished scroller.

Choosing the correct blade size and tooth style for the material to be cut is the key factor for accurate and smooth scroll sawing. If it is done right, one can eliminate or reduce the constant problem of sanding!

OLSON
Scroll Saw Blades
Selection Chart

Material | **Finish**

Recommended | Can Use | Not Recommended

Material columns: Hard Wood 1/2"–3/4" · Hard Wood to 1½" · Soft Wood to 1/2"–3/4" · Soft Wood to 1½" · Veneer/Thin Wood to 3/16" · Plywood · MDF · Particle Board · Corian 1/8"–1/2" · Plastic 1/2"–3/4" · Non Ferrous Metal · Aluminum
Finish columns: Smooth · Splinter-Free · Medium

Olson No.	Univ. No.	Width	Thickness	TPI/No. Rev.	Tooth Style	Pilot Hole	Application
PGT® Precision Ground Tooth (The Best!)							Skip Tooth PGT / Double Tooth PGT
455RG	5RG	.045"	.018"	12/9	Skip	1/16"	
457RG	7RG	.047"	.018"	10/7	Skip	1/16"	Ultra smooth finish,
459RG	9RG	.049"	.018"	8/6	Skip	1/16"	straight or close radius
495RG	5RG	.045"	.018"	12/8	Double	1/16"	cutting, splinter-free,
497RG	7RG	.047"	.018"	10.5/8	Double	1/16"	clean edges
499RG	9RG	.049"	.018"	9/6	Double	1/16"	
Crown Tooth™							
620	2/0	.024"	.011"	20	Crown	1/32"	Veining, line art, extreme radius cutting
622	2	.026"	.013"	20	Crown	3/64"	Extreme radius, delicate fretwork
623	3	.032"	.014"	16	Crown	3/64"	Tight radius fretwork
625	5	.038"	.016"	16	Crown	1/16"	Close radius fretwork, general purpose
627	7	.045"	.017"	11	Crown	1/16"	Close radius, general purpose
629	9	.053"	.018"	6	Crown	1/16"	General purpose, multi-layers
632	12	.065"	.024"	6	Crown	5/64"	Heavy duty for faster cuts
Reverse Tooth							
440R	2/0	.022"	.010"	28/21	Skip	1/32"	Veining, line art, extreme radius cutting
443R	2R	.029"	.012"	20/14	Skip	3/64"	Extreme radius, delicate fretwork
446R	5R	.038"	.016"	12.5/9	Skip	3/64"	Close radius fretwork, general purpose
448R	7R	.047"	.017"	11.5/8	Skip	1/16"	Close radius, general purpose
450R	9R	.054"	.019"	11.5/8	Skip	1/16"	General purpose, multi-layers
453R	12R	.062"	.024"	9.5/6	Skip	5/64"	Heavy duty for faster cuts
420R	–	.100"	.022"	9/5	Skip	1/8"	For cutting thick wood and multi-layers
Flat End Spiral							
468	2	–	.035"	41	–	5/64"	Medium speed and medium finish of hard and soft wood, plaster, and wallboard
469	4	–	.041"	36	–	7/64"	
Spiral							
461	0	–	.032"	46	–	3/64"	Bevel cut letters, etc.,
463	2	–	.035"	41	–	5/64"	medium finish fretwork and
465	4	–	.041"	36	–	7/64"	workpieces too large to turn

PGT® blades have razor sharp reverse teeth with widely spaced gullets for cutting straighter, faster, smoother, more accurately. PGT's minimize burning and provide the ultimate sand-free, splinterless finish with a clean edge. Double tooth style is especially good for cutting hard woods.

Hint! Reverse Tooth blades work best with 1-2 reverse teeth showing above the table on the upstroke! Adjust blade in holder or trim when necessary.

Unique **Crown Tooth** blades cut on both up and down strokes. Two way cutting action provides a smooth, splinterless finish, and clean edges. When worn, the blade can be turned over for cutting with a fresh set of teeth!

Hint! Tension blade properly! With reasonable force the center of the blade should not move more than 1/8" front to back. Too little tension weakens performance.

Reverse Tooth blades have skip style teeth and reverse teeth that eliminate underside tearout and provide a smooth, splinterless finish.

Hint! More teeth per inch provide a finer cut (good for soft wood). Less TPI provide a coarser cut (good for hard wood). Use the highest number blade for your application (larger blades are more durable).

Flat End Spiral blades are the same as our regular spiral blades, but with flat ends for easier blade installation and retention. Offered in the two most popular sizes.

Spiral blades saw in all directions with 360° cutting capability. Excellent for 0° radius scroll/fret work – no need to turn the workpiece. Bevel cut letters and numbers.

The Olson Saw Company, Bethel, CT 06801 USA

OLSON® Scroll Saw Blades
Selection Chart

Material columns (left to right): Hard Wood 1/2"–3/4" · Hard Wood to 1 1/2" · Soft Wood 1/2"–3/4" · Soft Wood to 1 1/2" · Veneer/Thin Wood to 3/16" · Plywood · MDF · Particle Board · Corian 1/8"–1/2" · Plastic 1/2"–3/4" · Non Ferrous Metal · Aluminum

Finish columns: Smooth · Splinter-Free · Medium

Legend: Recommended · Can Use · Not Recommended

Olson No.	Univ. No.	Width	Thickness	TPI/No. Rev.	Tooth Style	Pilot Hole	Application
Thick Wood							
408	–	.080"	.018"	7	Hook	3/32"	Thick wood – up to 2" without burning!
Skip Tooth							
400	3/0	.022"	.008"	33	Skip	1/32"	Ultra intricate sawing, veining, line art, close knit jig saw puzzles
440	2/0	.022"	.010"	28	Skip	1/32"	Extremely intricate sawing, veining, line art
443	2	.029"	.012"	20	Skip	3/64"	Tight radius work, fretwork
445	4	.035"	.015"	15	Skip	1/16"	Tight radius work, fretwork
446	5	.038"	.016"	12.5	Skip	1/16"	Close radius cutting
448	7	.045"	.017"	11.5	Skip	1/16"	General Purpose
450	9	.053"	.018"	11.5	Skip	1/16"	General Purpose
453	12	.062"	.024"	9.5	Skip	5/64"	Heavy duty for fast cuts
Pinned							
424P	–	.070"	.010"	18.5	Skip	3/16"	Skip style teeth/ Very thin cuts
405P	–	.110"	.018"	20	Reg.	3/16"	Regular style teeth/ thin cuts
410P	–	.100"	.018"	7	Hook	3/16"	Thick wood, up to 2" without burning!
411P	–	.110"	.018"	15	Reg.	3/16"	General purpose, regular style teeth
412P	–	.110"	.018"	10	Reg.	3/16"	Regular style teeth, fast cutting
420RP	–	.110"	.018"	9/5	Skip	3/16"	Heavy duty widely-spaced set teeth for fast cutting
Double Tooth							
432	3/0	.023"	.008"	33	Dbl.	1/32"	Ultra intricate sawing, veining, line art, close knit jig saw puzzles
433	2/0	.023"	.011"	37	Dbl.	1/32"	Veining, line art & marquetry
434	1	.026"	.013"	30	Dbl.	3/64"	Delicate fretwork
435	3	.032"	.014"	23	Dbl.	3/64"	Extremely intricate sawing
436	5	.038"	.016"	16	Dbl.	1/16"	Tight radius work
437	7	.044"	.018"	13	Dbl.	1/16"	Close radius cutting
438	9	.053"	.018"	11	Dbl.	1/16"	General purpose
439	12	.061"	.022"	10	Dbl.	5/64"	Heavy duty, fast cuts
Metal Cutting							
485	–	.041"	.019"	30	Reg.	–	Very thin metal sheets
487	–	.049"	.022"	25	Reg.	–	Thin metal sheets
490	–	.070"	.023"	20	Reg.	–	Thicker metal sheets

Hint! (All Blades) For best performance, use lower numbers for thinner stock and higher numbers for thicker stock.

Skip tooth blades are excellent for fast cuts that provide smooth finishes and good chip clearance.

Hint! (All Blades) For best performance, use lower numbers for tighter radii and higher numbers for more general purpose cuts.

Pinned scroll saw blades are for machines that require 5" pinned blades. They are perfect for Sears Craftsman, Penn State, Delta, Ryobi and all 15" and 16" imported scroll saws that require pinned blades.

Hint! Slow feed rate down! Relax! Let the blade do the cutting to minimize burning. Also, use a lube stick on the blade or clear shipping tape on the workpiece to inhibit scorching.

Double tooth blades have two teeth together followed by a flat space for efficient chip removal. They cut fast, leaving clean edges in wood and plastic.

Metal cutting blades have more teeth per inch required for cutting thin metal and other hard materials.

The Olson Saw Company, Bethel, CT 06801 USA

© Copyright 2000 Olson Saw Co.

OL-1052 n 5/00

Sizing, Copying, & Transferring the Pattern

• **Sizing & Copying the Pattern:** Use a photocopier to make several copies of the particular pattern you wish to cut out. Modify them to your satisfaction, by either enlarging them or reducing them to suit your needs.

The photocopied pattern.

Cut the pattern straight along the base. This is important for proper alignment with the wood. If the bottom of the pattern is straight, it can be laid against the straight edge of the wood to give you a clean line for joining later.

Cut roughly around the rest of the pattern.

• **Transferring the Pattern to the Work Piece.** There are several products on the market one can choose to adhere the pattern to the work piece. They include: Glue Stic™ by Avery, 3M's Scotchbrand™ spray adhesive, rubber cement, etc. Make sure they are the repositionable or temporary bond items.

Two of the adhesives you may use for the piece.

Glue the pattern to the wood.

Selection of Materials

The provided patterns may be sawed from a wide variety of different materials & different thickness—the choices are entirely yours. The range can include wood products, plastic, or even metals.

I am using two hard woods, maple and walnut, for their contrasting colors.

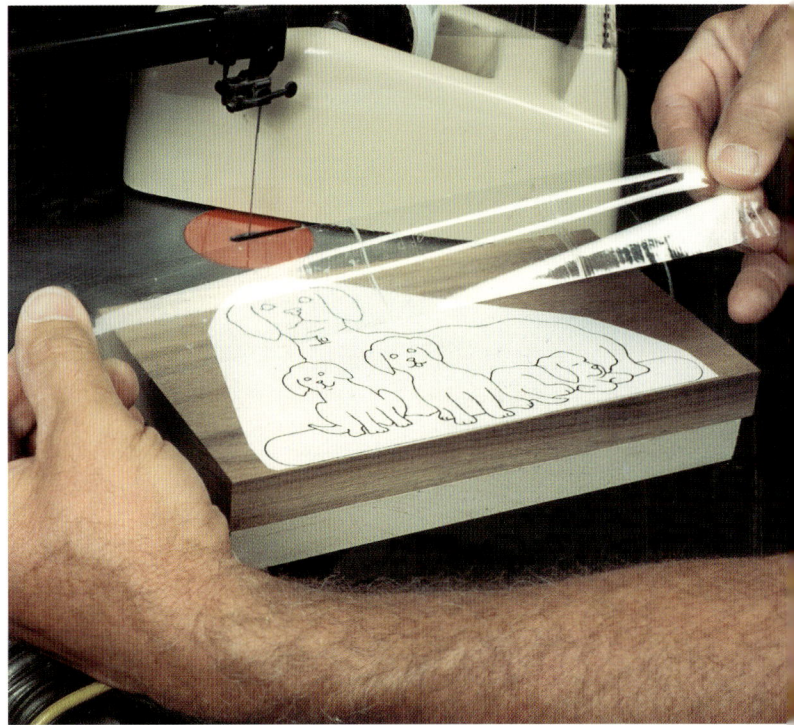

To hold the two pieces of wood together I use clear packing tape. As mentioned earlier, this has the added benefit of lubricating the blade as it cuts, keeping it from burning the wood.

They are the roughly the same dimensions, with identical thicknesses. These are 3/4" thick.

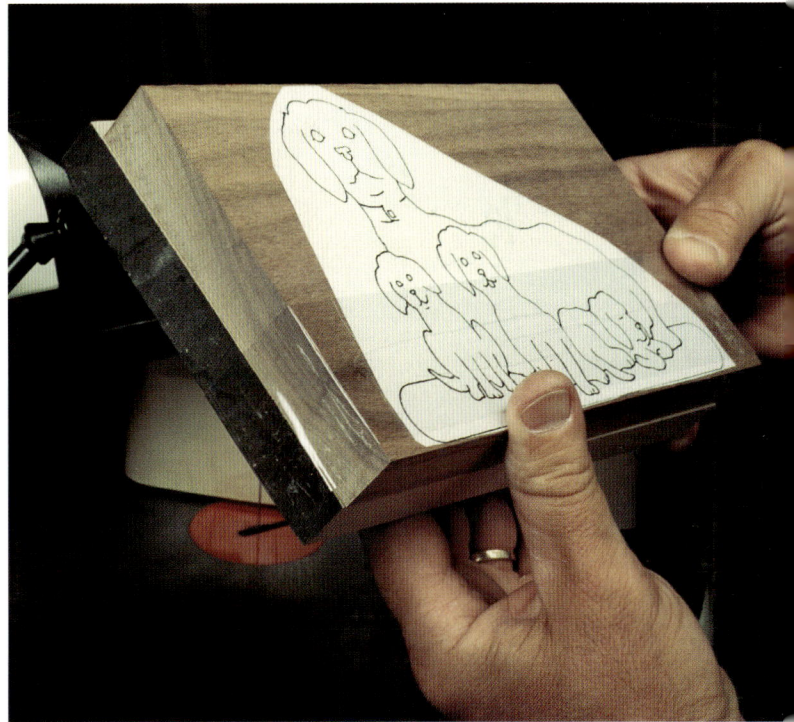

I run the tape around all sides of the wood…

Until the piece is encased in tape.

Scroll Saw Cutting Preparation

• **Wax the work table** periodically. This will help the stock slide easily over the work table for better control.

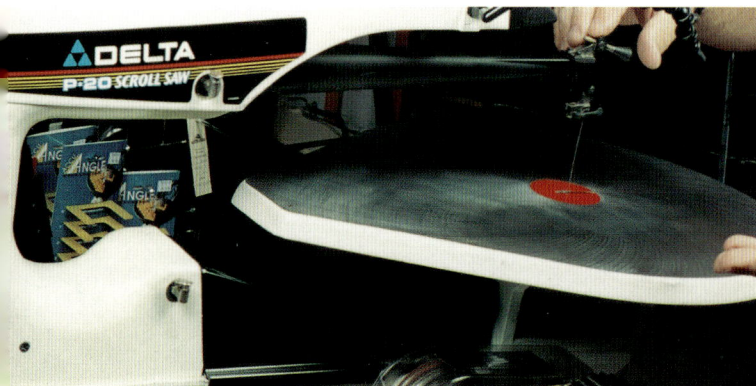

For this project I am using a Delta P-20 Scroll Saw. It was the newest available and is the most user-friendly scroll saw on the market. It has numerous features, including a belt drive, that make almost vibration free.

Periodically I wax the table surface using a spray wax.

• **Level the table**, and, using a square, check to see if the blade is at an angle of 90 degrees or perpendicular to the saw table.

Tables can be readily adjusted to establish level.

• **Select the blade**. Remember, use the right blade for the right material. For guidance, check out the blade use Guideline Chart in this book.

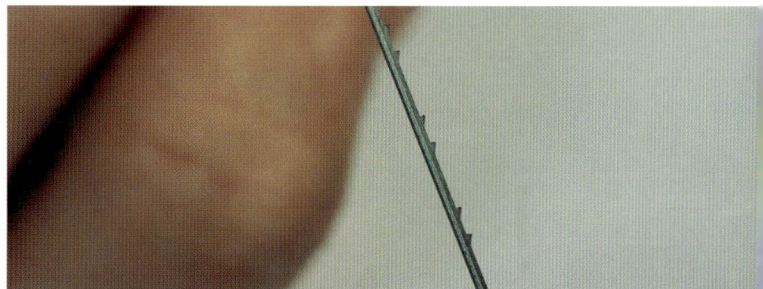

The blade for this hardwood project is the Olson PGT double reverse tooth. It clears chips easily and runs cooler.

• **Check blade tension.** The Rule of Thumb: When you push the blade front to back with your thumb, you should get a 1/8" deflection. Remember periodically blade tension adjustment is a must.

• **Decide on a cutting speed.** Establish the proper "SPM," Strokes Per Minute, for the project. Check out the General Guide to Cutting Speed for the materials you have selected. Remember to read the section pertaining to special blade and cutting hints; as well as the right blade for the right job, To some sawyers this will truly be helpful.

• **Don't be afraid.** Learn not to be afraid of the scroll saw blade and work from 1/2" to 1" around the scroll saw blade while you are cutting. This is most important, and will make a BIG difference on your finish product.

Maintenance & Upkeep of your Scroll Saw

All scroll saws require periodic maintenance. This includes:
• Greasing (not oiling) of pivot bolts every 50-75 hours of running time. Note: On the new delta P-20 you have no choice but to oil.
• Checking your motor brushes periodically and replacing them as needed.
• Visually checking belts and or other wearing parts.
• Waxing the work table frequently.
• Cleaning the scroll saw periodically, especially around the motor & electronic controls. Compressed air works well for this task.

Safety Procedures

Read your owners operating manual is essential for all sawyers. Once again take care and truly enjoy your scroll saw.

General Characteristic &Manufacturing Processes of Scroll Saw Blades

- Material: Carbon: .070%-.079%   Silicone: 0.10%-.030%
                     Manganese: 0.30%-0.70% Chromium: 0.10%
- Hardness: RC 53-55
- Style
    (skip tooth): 15.0 TPI
- Dimension
    (tooth cut):   .001"/.008"
- Bend Test: The Reverse Tooth Fret saw blade must be able to revolve around a 360º pin
                     without fracturing. Then the blade must return to its relaxed state and remain bent.

All the carbon steel wire product produced in the U.S. today either comes from an open hearth or electric furnaces. The typical USA Acid Bessemer Process is what produces the superior quality grades of steel. Virtually all scroll saw and similar blades are manufactured from a non-resulphurized high carbon steel.

- Scroll Blades Regular Style Teeth (5"or6"): Blades are notched & set.
- Skip Tooth Fret, Saw Blades (5"): Blades are milled with no set.
- Reverse Skip Tooth Saw Blades (5"): Blades are milled with no set.
- Double Tooth Fret Saw Blades (5")—Blades are milled with no set.
- Metal Cutting Saw Blades (5"): Blades are milled with no set.
- Spiral Saw Blades (5"): Blades are milled with no set.
- PGT Saw Blades (5"): Blades are precision ground with no set.
- Double Tooth PGT Saw Blades (5"): Blades are precision ground with no set.
- Thick wood Saw Blades (5"): Blades are notched and set.

Note: for the experts out there NOTCHED BLADES are extremely sharp and can be equal to a milled or precision ground tooth blade.

Pozsgai's Designs' General Guide to Cutting Speed (SPM)

	APPLICATION	SPEED (SPM)
SOFT WOODS	High speed quickly & easily cuts pines, balsa wood, bass wood, plywood, cedar, fir and others	1600-2000
HARDWOODS	For making intricate cuts on cherry, walnut, oak, teak, ash, maple, purple heart, rosewood and others without burning wood. With stock that is 3/4" & above use the 3M tape trick.	1400-2000
METALS	Slow speed keeps blades cool to minimize breakage. Can cut brass, copper, aluminum, soft 16 to 20 gauge low carbine steel sheet stock and others.	400-700
PLASTICS	Slow speed helps to prevent melting of some cast acrylic, ASB, lexan & Plexiglas. Note: An extruded acrylic can be cut easily at 1500-1700 SPM	300-1000

The Project

Sawing Out the Pattern

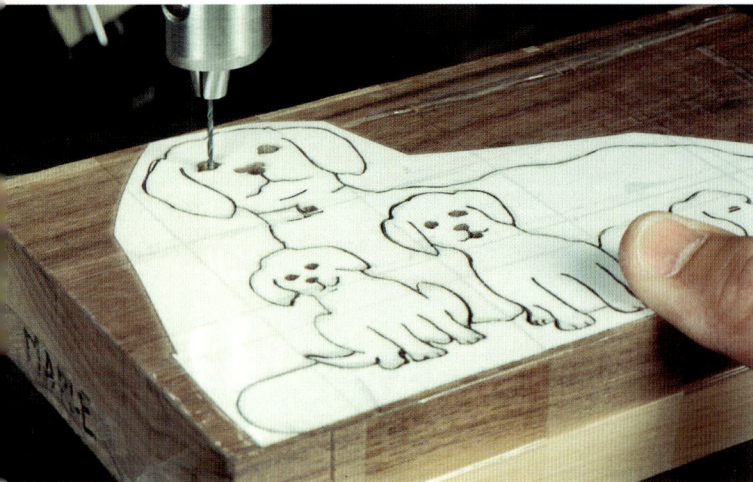

I generally begin by drilling out the eyes, nose, and other areas that can be best formed with a drill press.

The result should be two identical figures, one in maple and one in walnut.

If properly aligned, the base should not need to be cut. Start at a corner of pattern and cut the outline. Then go back and cut the detail lines within the pattern.

Each segment of the pattern should be independent. In this case the pillow, pups and mother are all completely cut out.

When the pattern is completely cut, remove the tape and the pattern.

The base is 3/4" to 1" stock. Since I have produced two patterns, I also will need two bases, one in maple and one in walnut.

Glue in place.

For the edge I am using an ogee fillet bit with two flutes and a bearing guide. I have decided to make these into pen holders, and have created a trough for the pen using a 1/2" box core bit.

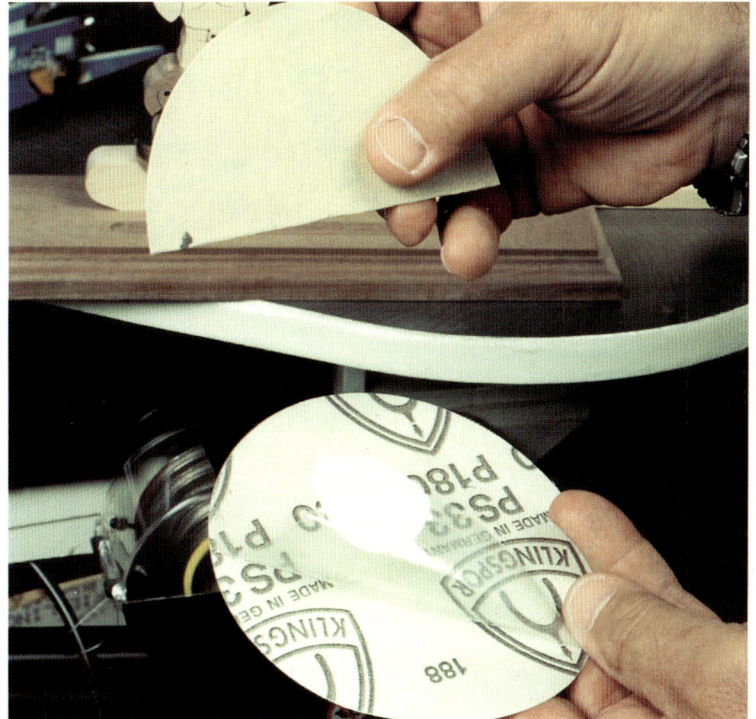

For sanding I use a 220 grit adhesive pad. I remove the back and fold the pad in half. Between finish coats I use a 320 grit pad.

Mix and arrange the pieces in an appealing way.

Finishing the Cutouts

There are numerous ways to finish your project depending on the pattern you choose, the type of material you'll use, and including what style you want to present it. They include natural finishes, stains, paints, and lacquers. The choice is strictly a matter of personal preference.

In the front you can see a finished piece. I use felt pads on the bottom to complete the piece.

Ways to Utilize Patterns

With the variety of positions, woods, and setting, one can be very creative in utilizing these patterns. A few ideas include:

• **Pictures.** This is done by simply adding a backing & frame.
• **Pen & Pencil Sets.** As we did here, all you need is an attractive base.

• **Refrigerator Magnets.** Place a magnet on the back and you have something beautiful to hold all those important messages and memories.
• **Clock Sets.** Quartz movements are readily available and easy to use.

For these possibilities and more, see the gallery that follows.

This pen holder would make a wonderful fixture in the office or the perfect gift.

14

The Gallery

Ornamental Patterns

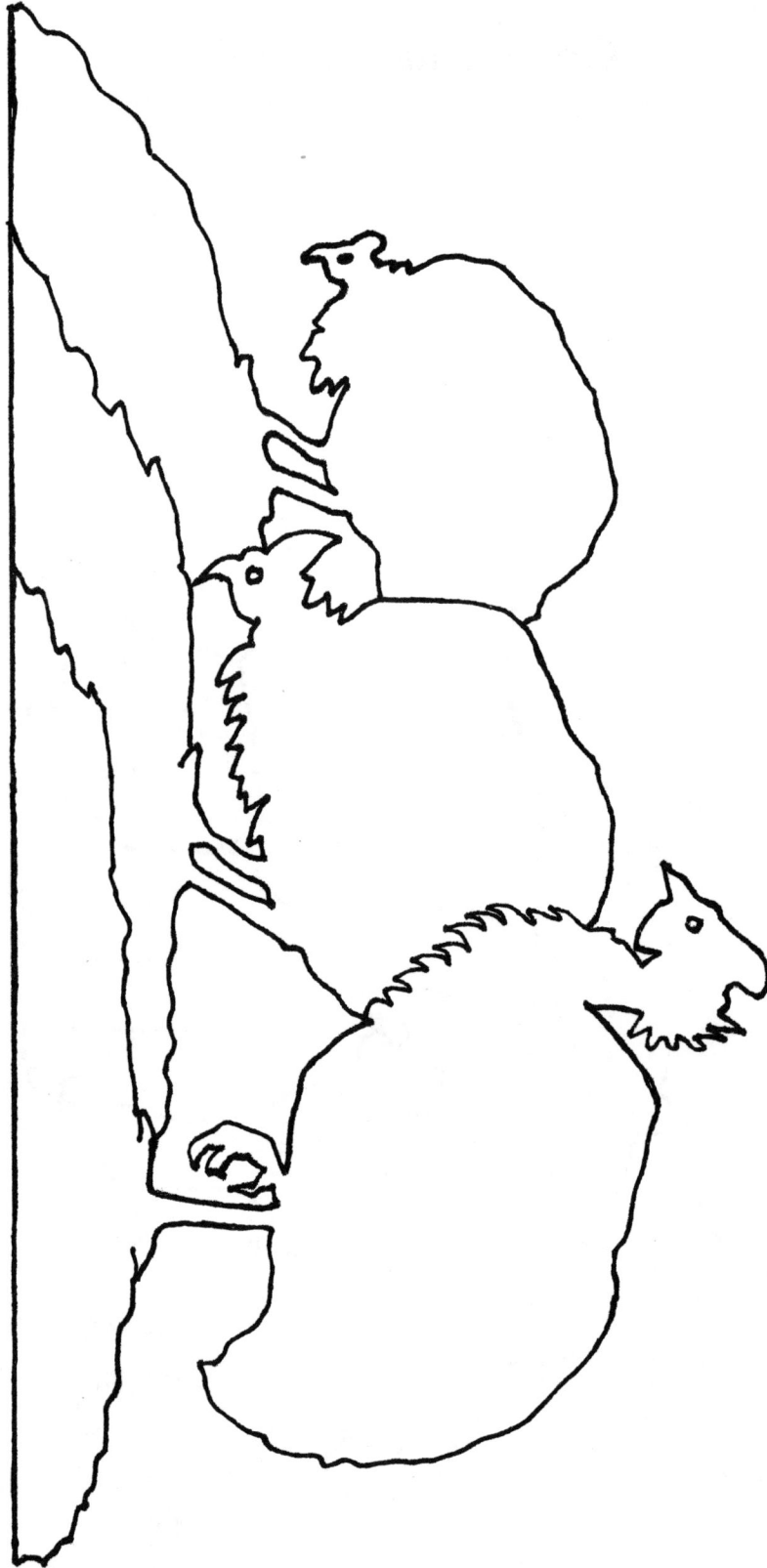

Guineafowl

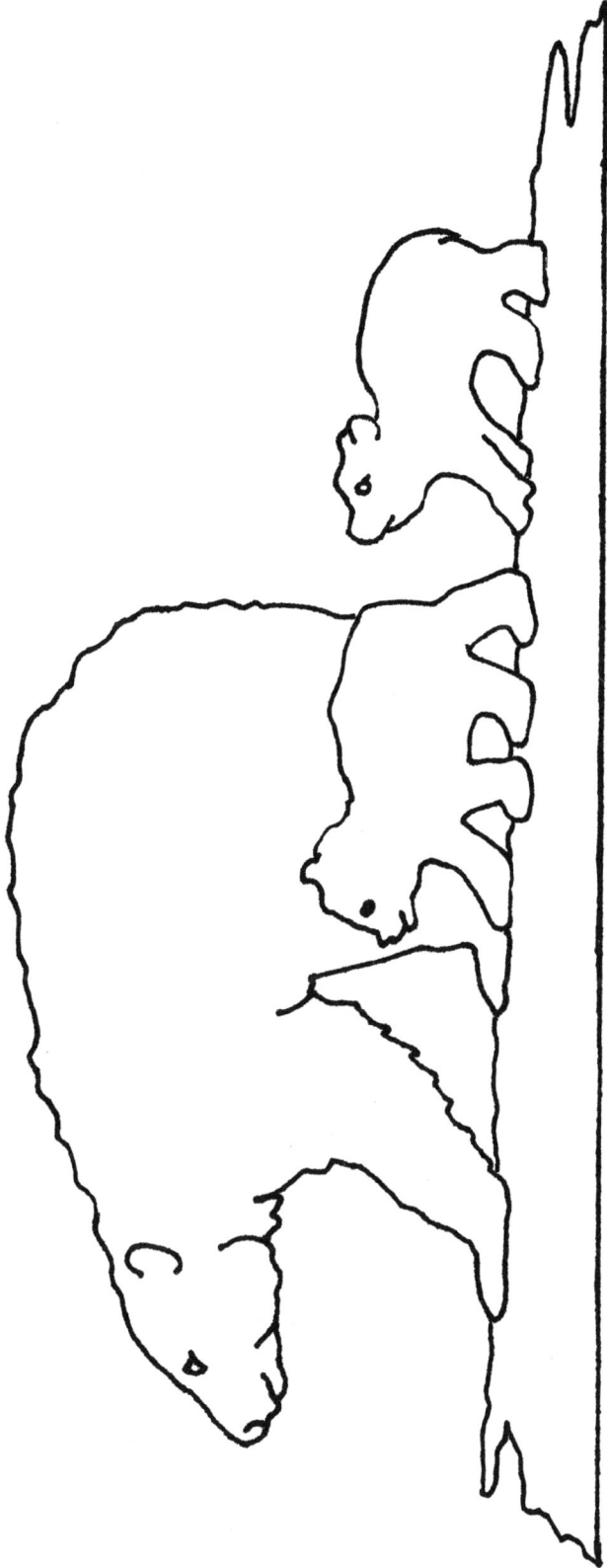

Deer

Greater Kudu

24

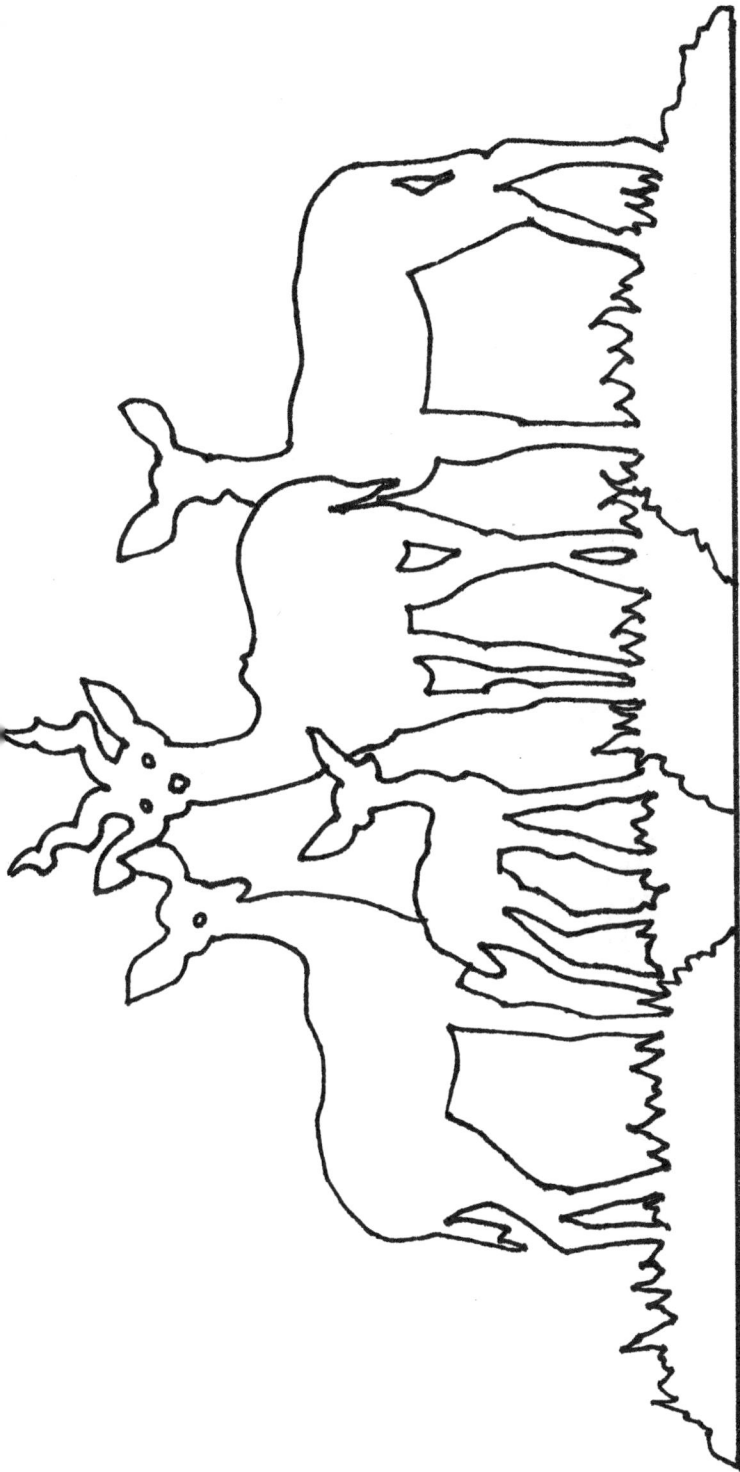
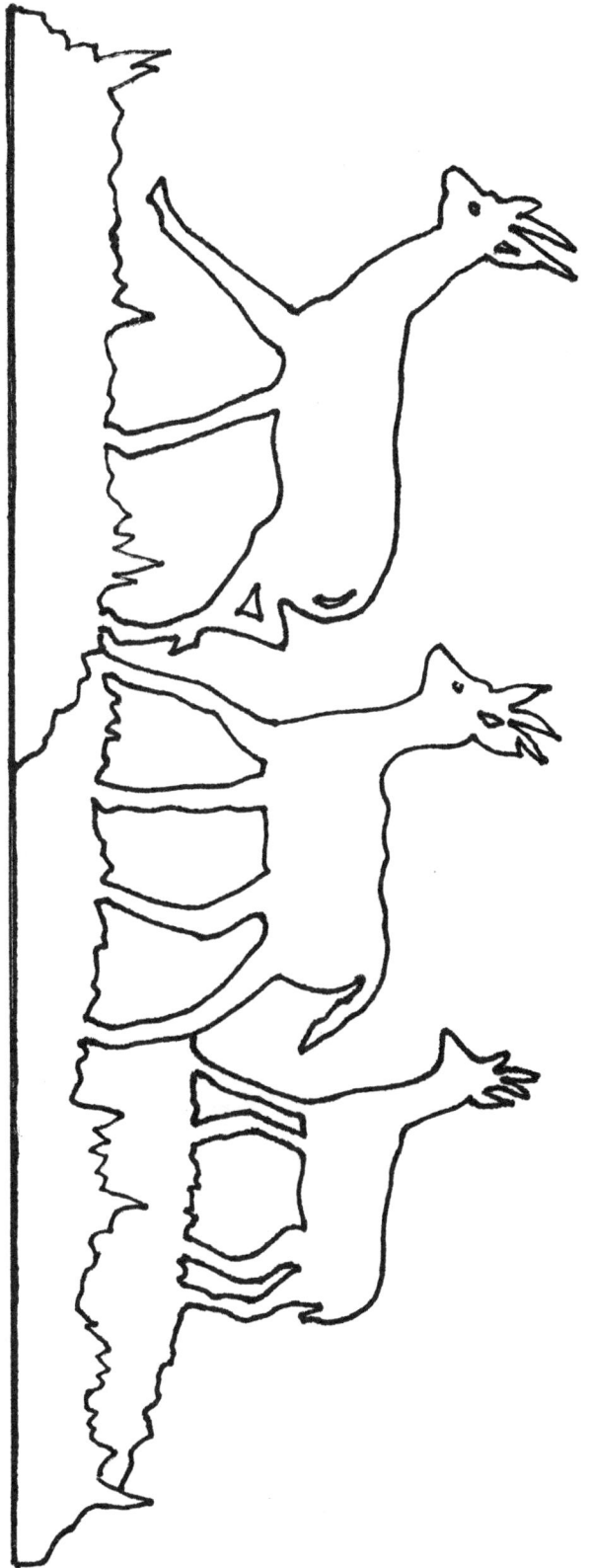

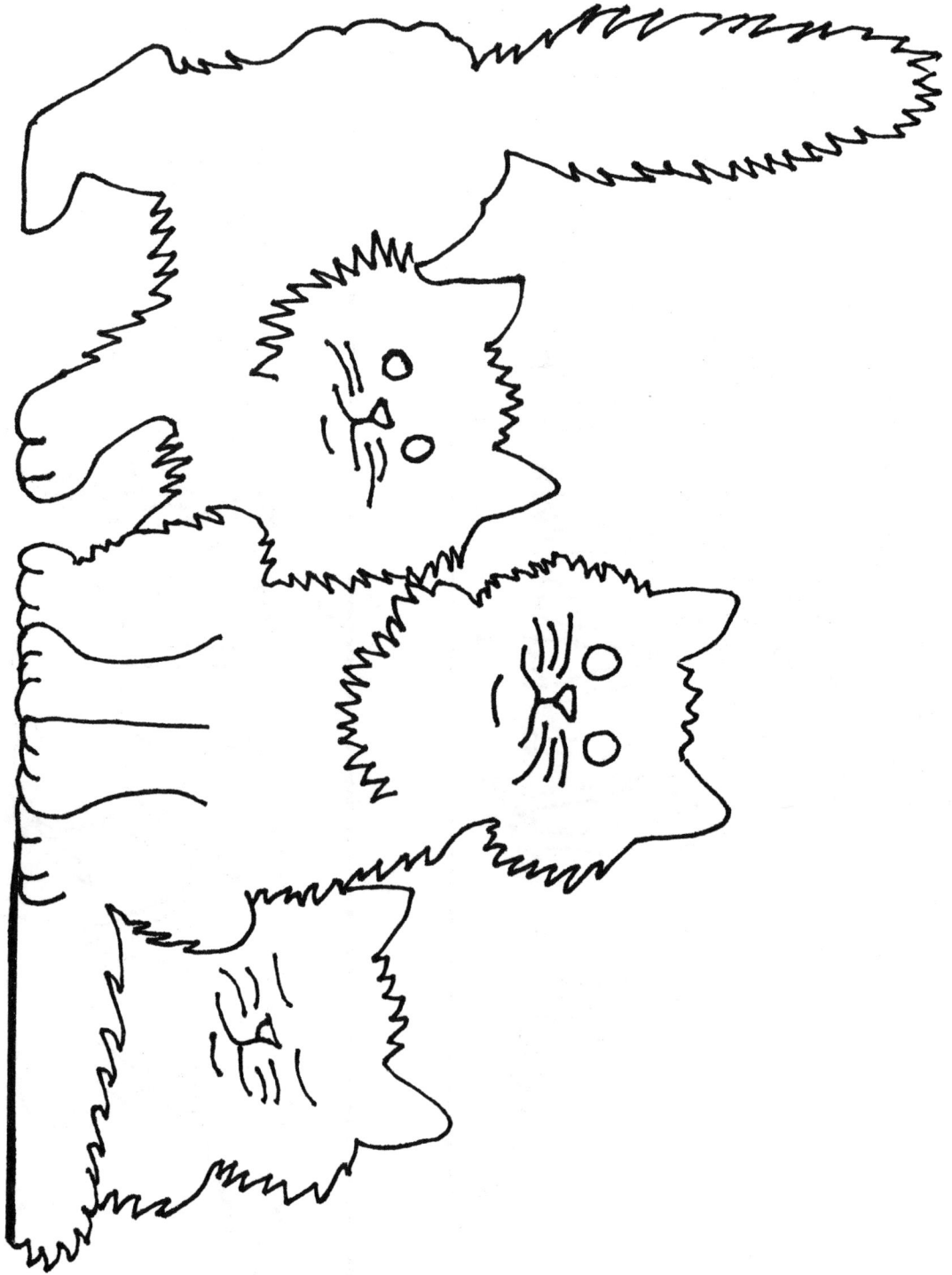

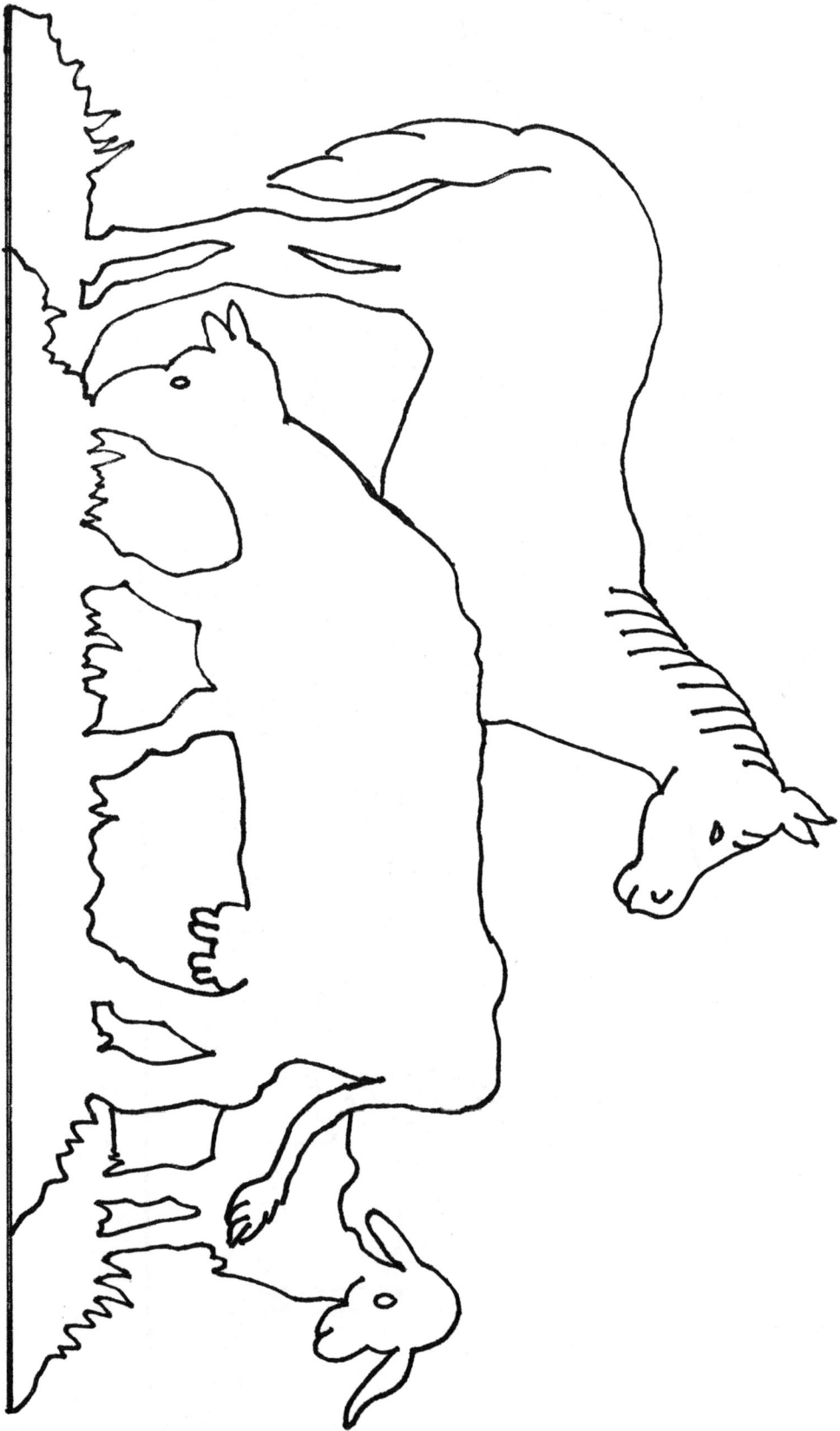

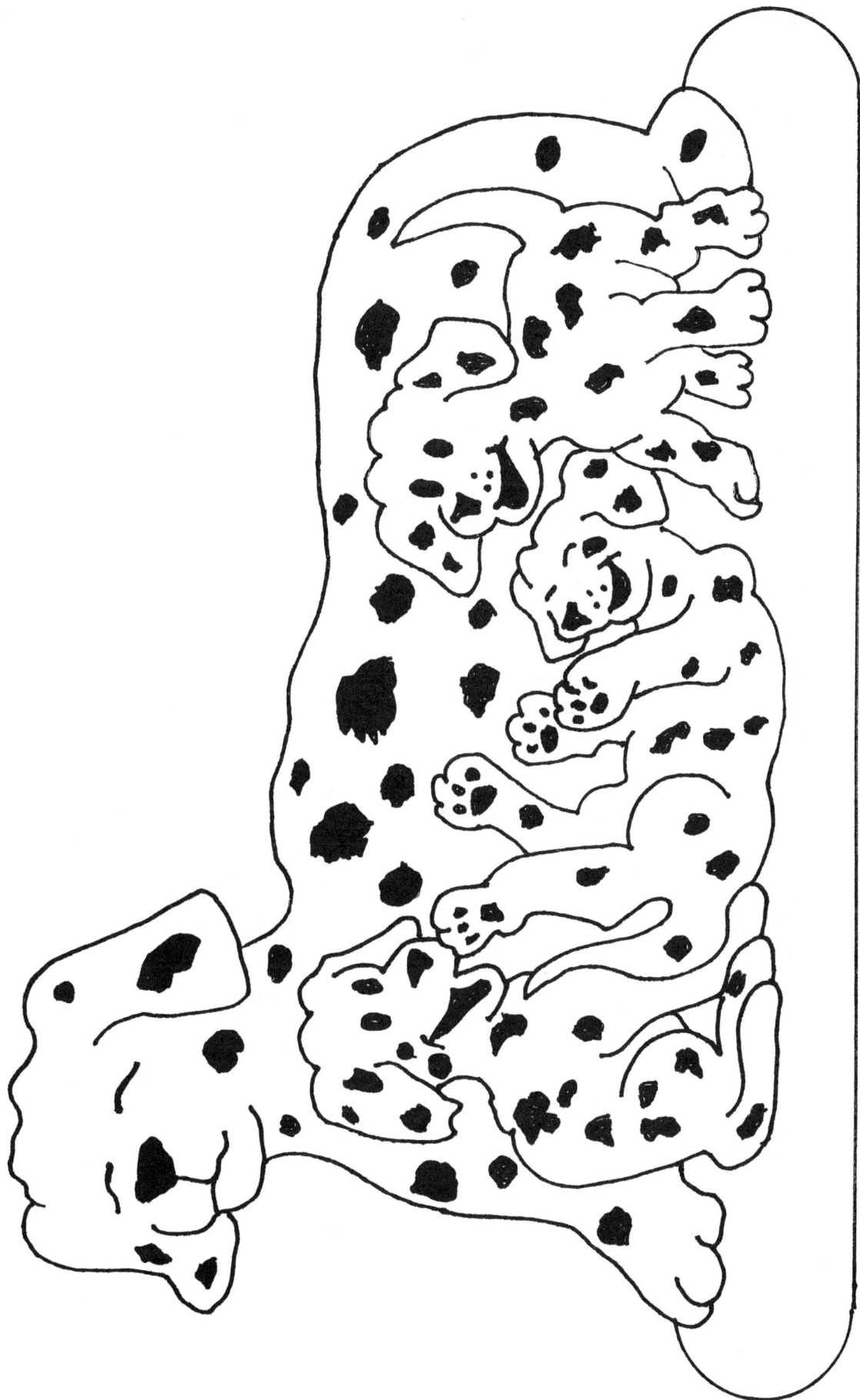

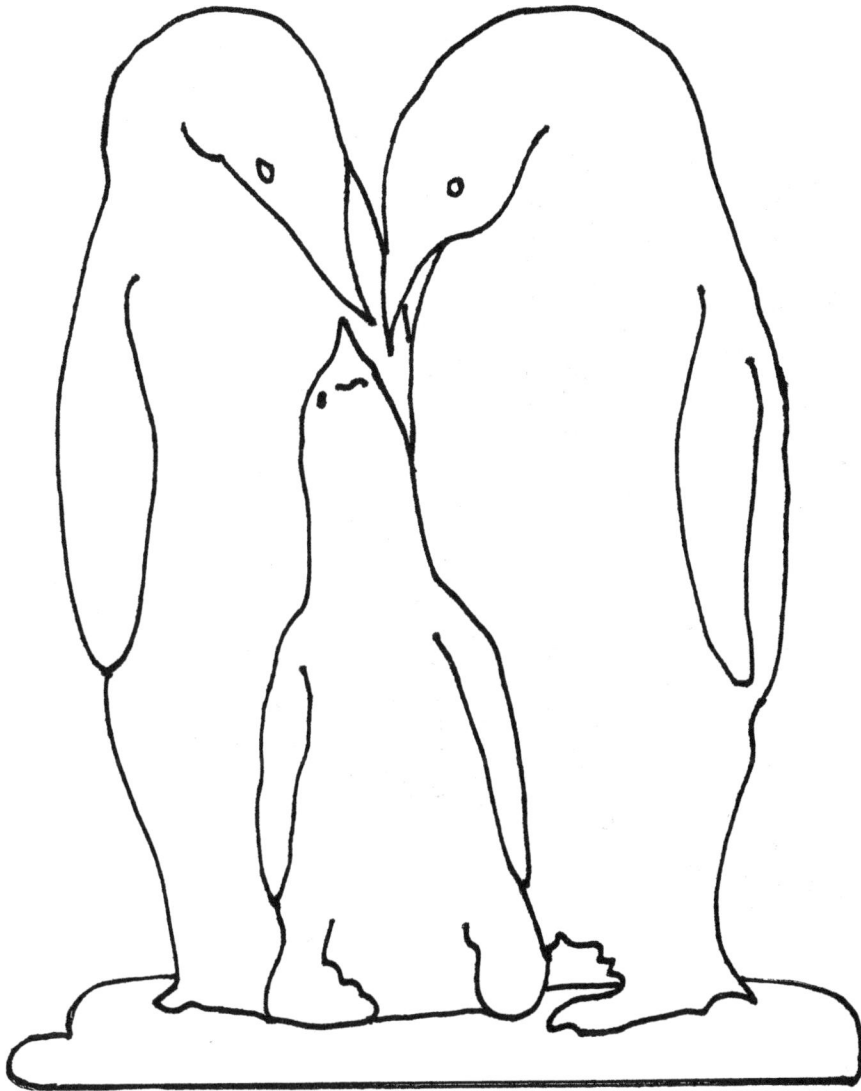

Bears

Cape Buffalo

41

Oryx

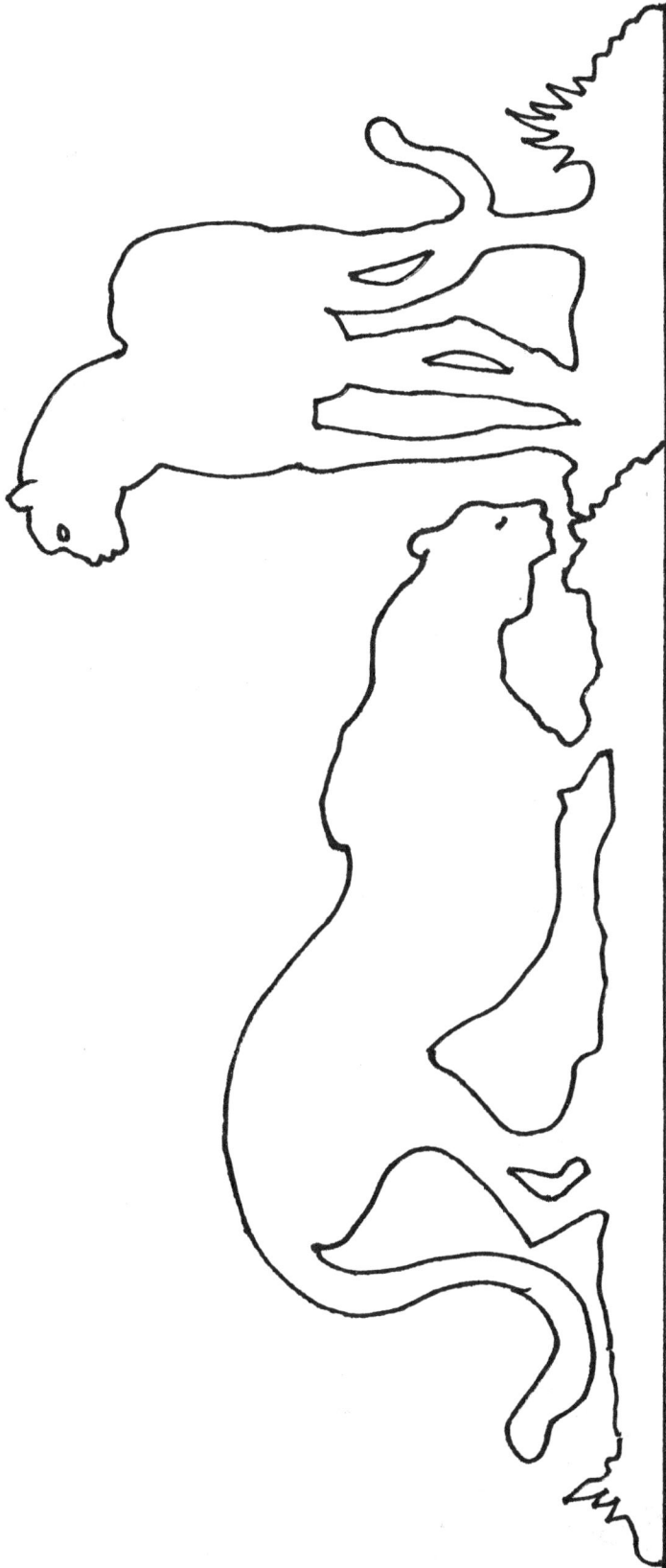

Whales

Hyenas

Sample Base Mounting Patterns

The various mounting bases are designed to give you an option and style to choose from for your project. Merely enlarge them to your desired needs. Remember to mix the various patterns with different woods to complement your art when using a base to mount on.

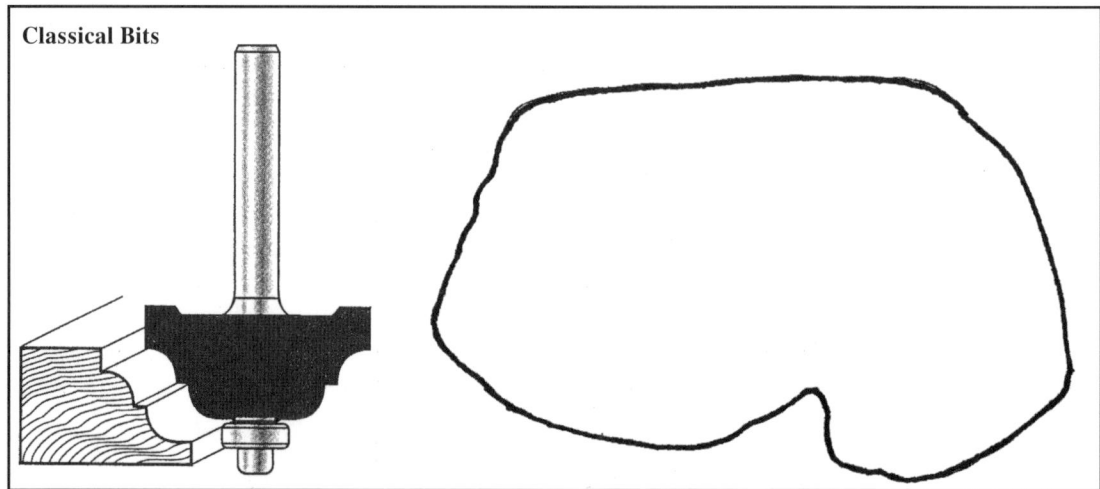

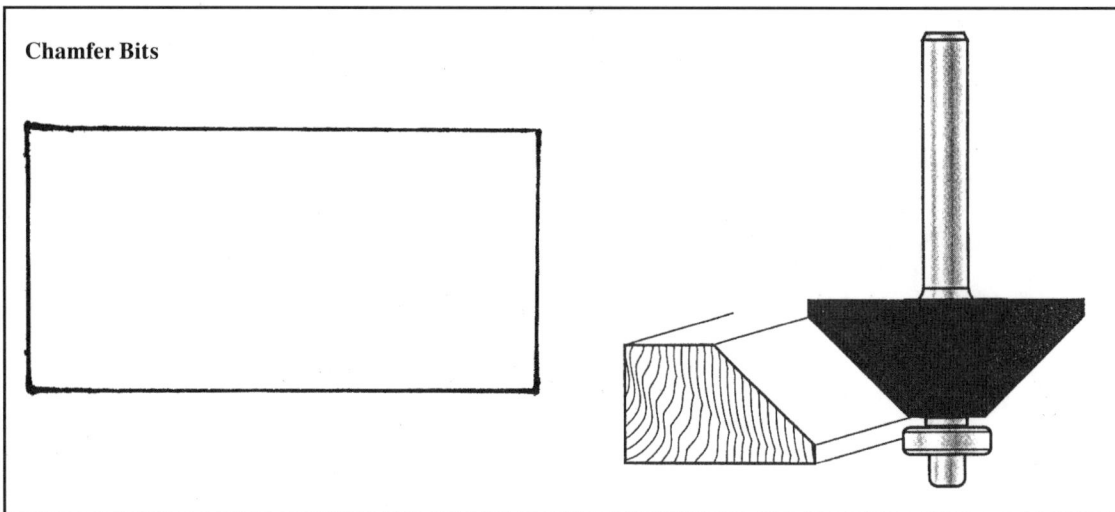

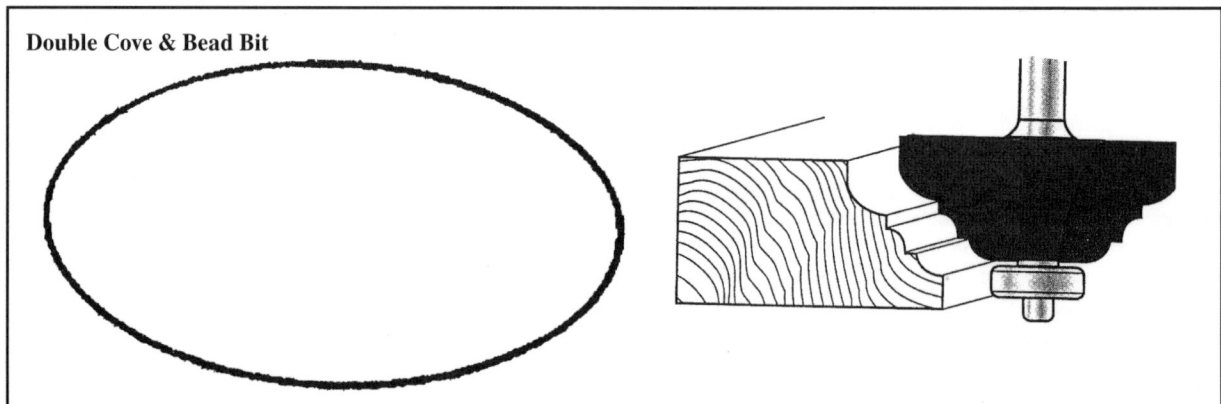

Classical Bits

Chamfer Bits

Double Cove & Bead Bit

Beading Bits

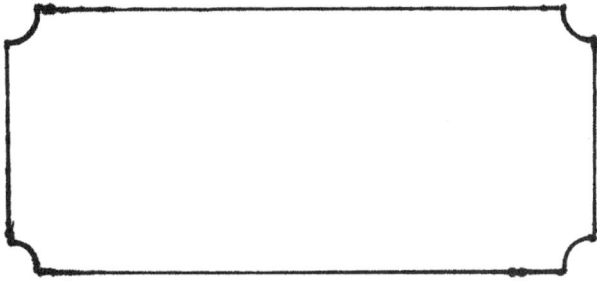

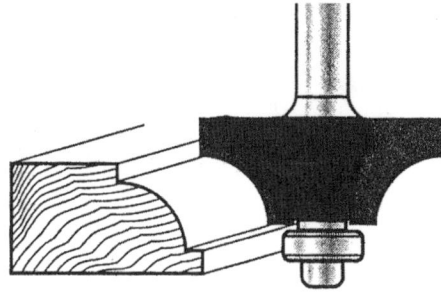

Double Round Over Bits

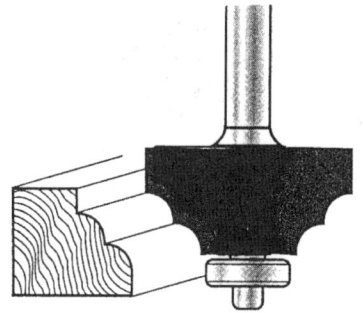

Ogee Fillet Bits

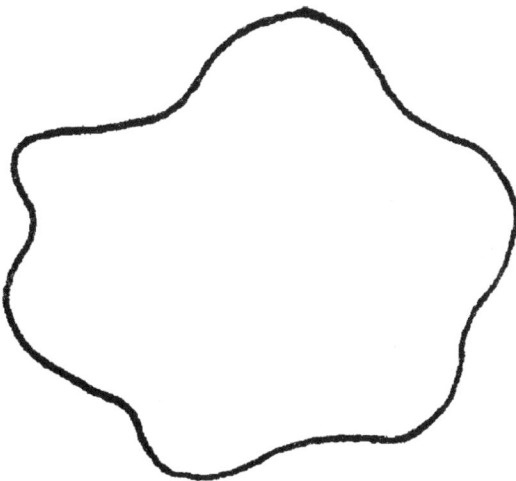

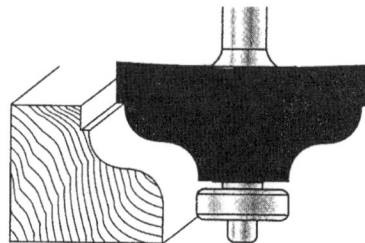

Alternative Router Bits and Profiles

Core Box Bits

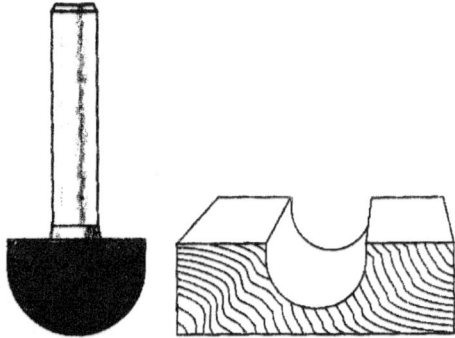

Cove & Bead Bits

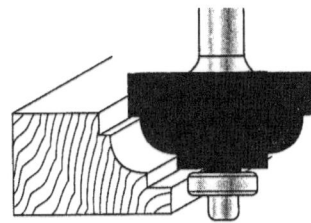

Roman Ogee Bits

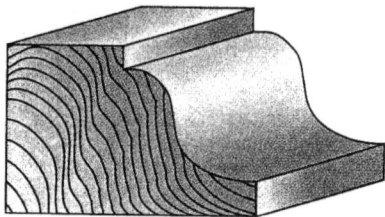

Cove Bits

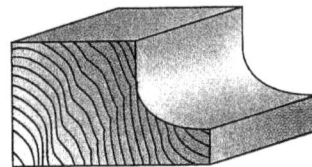

Round Over Bits

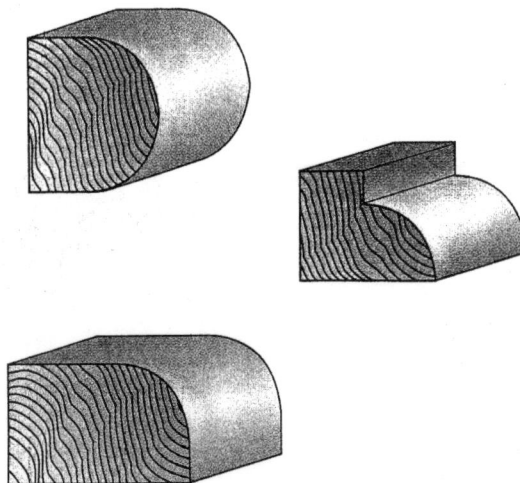